THE LIFE OF SAINT JOHN VIANNEY, THE CURE OF ARS

WITH A NOVENA AND LITANY

ANONYMOUS

CATHOLIC WAY
PUBLISHING

Copyright © 1911 by Joseph Schaefer, New York, US.
Retypeset and republished in 2013 by Catholic Way Publishing.
Cover design by Catholic Way Publishing.

NIHIL OBSTAT:
THOMAS B. COTTER, PH.D.
Censor.

IMPRIMATUR:
JOHN M. FARLEY
Archbishop of New York
October 22, 1910.

5" x 8" Paperback. Also available as an E-Book.
Kindle: ISBN-13: 978-1-78379-230-6
EPUB: ISBN-13: 978-1-78379-231-3

This work is published for the greater Glory of Jesus Christ through His most Holy Mother Mary and for the sanctification of the militant Church and her members.

10 9 8 7 6 5 4 3 2 1

ISBN-13: 978-1-78379-229-0

ISBN-10: 1-78379-229-9

CATHOLICWAYPUBLISHING.COM
LONDON, UK
2013

TABLE OF CONTENTS

PREFACE

Spiritual reading has always been encouraged by our Holy Mother Church, because it strengthens our faith and stimulates us to be more devout in the practice of our religion. The materialistic tone and trend of most modern literature, however, makes the reading and dissemination of Catholic books all the more urgent and necessary at the present time.

The mind is moulded largely by reading and good minds were never more needed than to-day, to combat the effects of the mental poison, which is daily absorbed by young and old through the medium of degrading literature. True, there are issued good books and periodicals which are not strictly religious in tone, but which, nevertheless, have a salutary influence upon the reader's mind. Their number, however, is comparatively small.

Good spiritual reading should not be made merely an infrequent departure from the reading of every day literature, but should be indulged in regularly and systematically by the Catholic laity in general.

Good books play an important part in fostering the early evidences of vocation. The youth, under their influence, voluntarily moves nearer to the goal of his aspirations, unforced by the caprice of the thoughtless or over-enthusiastic parents. Numerous little incidents are associated with the life of Blessed Jean Baptist Vianney, which will help to develop the germ of sacerdotal vocation.

The young seminarian will find Vianney's life to be a genuine exhortation which will operate to fortify him in the face of trials and temptation.

The priest himself, who aims to acquire all the graces which may bless the priesthood, may justly take pleasure in imitating the virtues, zeal, piety and charity of the humble cure of Ars.

The little volume describes in simple language the life of a man, who, in our own time, earned by his holiness, acts of self-sacrifice, self-abnegation and miracles, wrought through the intervention of God, the blessings of beatification.

Vianney's life may be read with profit by everyone. The descriptions of his toils and sufferings in behalf of his fellow-men, and his efforts to save souls, cannot fail to inspire the reader with uplifting thoughts.

Editor's Note: Please bear in mind that, while reading this book, references to 'Blessed' John Vianney are obsolete, as he has been raised to Sainthood in 1925, by Pope Pius XI.

ALBERT A. LINGS.

INTRODUCTION

ON January 8, 1905, John Baptist Marie Vianney, that most humble of country curates, was admitted by our Holy Father, Pope Pius X, into the glorious ranks of the beatified of the Catholic Church. And in very truth that devoted guardian of souls had well merited the exalted distinction thus conferred; for, during the forty-two years of his holy life, countless thousands had come under the influence of his active and untiring zeal, and were guided by him in the way of their salvation.

The fame of the gentle "Cure of Ars" has long since passed the boundaries of his native land, and the fact that his name has been officially promulgated for veneration is sufficient reason for presenting this noble personality to the attention of the Catholics of English speaking countries. We do this with the greater pleasure, since in thus seeking to promote the honor of the blessed cure we are at one with our Holy Father, who constantly keeps his statue before him upon his desk in the Vatican palace.

Thereby Pius X, himself, manifests his high regard for the blessed one and confirms the words pronounced shortly before the beatification of the former humble cure. Upon that occasion the Holy Father said: "We can hardly give befitting expression to the joy of our soul whilst we make public the solemn decree which affirms the validity of the miracles worked by God through the intercession of the venerable John Baptist Vianney. For our part, during the many years that we have exercised the pastoral office with affectionate solicitude, nothing more agreeable has taken place, or could occur, than to behold this venerable cure elevated to the number of the blessed in the Catholic Church."

Vianney was a truly apostolic guardian of souls. And because he lived so near our own time, the history of his life-work becomes all the more valuable and interesting. The present sketch, designed only as an outline, is necessarily brief and gives but a meagre description of the virtues, the mortifications, the zeal and the ceaseless activities of the blessed cure. Those desiring a more extended history of the life of this great man are referred to the work of the Abbe Alfred Monnin, his friend and fellow laborer.

Brief and unassuming, however, as this present narration may be, we put it forth in the hope that it may contribute, in some degree, to make known the merits of this distinguished servant of God, and in order that those who read it may be prompted to follow the counsels and imitate the example of his saintly life.

CHAPTER I

CHILDHOOD AND YOUTH OF THE SAINTLY CURE

⚜

JEAN Baptist Marie Vianney, afterwards to become famous as the cure of Ars, was born May 8th, 1786, at Dardilly, in the South of France, not far from the City of Lyons, and was the fourth child of humble country folks.

His father, Mathieu Vianney, and his mother, Marie Beluse, possessed some land adjoining their simple dwelling. Despite the fact that they were not rich they practiced the greatest hospitality toward the poor and needy. With joyful wonder the youthful Jean beheld, evening after evening, a number of poor and needy wayfarers entertained at the family meal. Not infrequently the elder Vianney would bestow his own share upon some belated arrival. This noble example made a profound impression upon the boy's pious disposition. Of his own accord he would go out to greet the needy travelers, opening the door for them and otherwise assisting them, and would even carry their torn garments to his mother, in order that she might mend them. By other kindly service he showed his sympathy with the poor and distressed who made their way to his father's house.

Jean had imbibed a love of piety with his mother's milk. The names of Jesus and Mary were the very first words to pass his baby lips. The first movement of his little hands, taught him by his mother, was to make the sign of the cross. Even as a child of four or five years Jean would retire to a place of solitude where, as the record says, "he spoke with the angel guardian."

As he grew up he occupied himself with the work of the farm, minding the cattle and doing other humble work. When in after years his name was mentioned with pious admiration by numberless Christians, Father Vianney was wont to recall his early years, saying:

"How happy was I, when I only had to care for my three sheep and my donkey. Then indeed I could pray to God according to my heart's desire."

Just as the boy arrived at the age of reason the churches of France, in consequence of the outbreak of the Revolution, were closed, and the priests banished. This was a severe trial for so devout a child, for at that early age he was sensible of the high importance of the Apostolic teaching, and in his eagerness to promote the love of God he gathered the village children about him and preached impressive sermons to them in his simple but earnest way.

The young missionary became acquainted in those evil days with many worthy priests, men who counted the threats and fury of the revolutionary heroes as nothing, when it was a question of saving souls and so unnoticed the fervent desire took possession of the boy's soul that he might one day be a priest and work for the glory of God and the salvation of souls. It was during those darkest hours for the Church in France, that Jean, with a number of other children, met in private to be prepared for the reception of his First Holy Communion. With what holy rapture did he approach the table of the Lord. That event was ever held in cherished remembrance by all who participated in it.

Many years elapsed from the day the youth received his First Holy Communion to that other day when he began his studies for the priesthood. Divine Providence willed, first of all, that his piety should be trained under the guidance of his good and worthy parents. His daily work was divided between prayer and work, or, to speak more correctly, his work was a continuous prayer. The life of his Divine Master, with its miracles and sufferings, supplied him with inexhaustible material for meditation. At the close of the day's work and in the company of his mother and sister Catherine, he read the Holy Scriptures and the lives of the Saints.

Being an extremely diligent and painstaking worker, and because of his uniform meekness of character, he was a great favorite at home as well as among his companions outside. Even upon boys who took no pains to be good, Jean's purity of heart made such an impression that they would cease their disedifying conversation whenever he approached.

Meanwhile Jean had hoped and prayed that he might become a priest, but he completed his seventeenth year without having yet begun his education so necessary to the fulfillment of his desire. Such a result seemed to be all the more impossible of accomplishment inasmuch as his father declared point-blank that he had no money to spare for his son's education.

In 1805, however, a ray of light appeared. The churches were re-opened following the conclusion of the concordat, and the Rev. Father Bailey, one of the zealous missionaries of the period, was appointed pastor of Ecully, a village adjacent to Dardilly. One of his early works was the establishment of a seminary for the education of youth for the priesthood. With his father's approval, Jean, then 19 years old, presented himself to Father Bailey. The latter had been aware for a long time of the young man's great piety, received him most kindly and admitted him as a student.

Thus it came about that Jean sat in class with boys much younger than he was. Had he been under instruction sooner it would not have been so very hard for him to learn, as he had a fair capacity for ordinary studies. But because he was only beginning at an age when most youths have already mastered the rudiments, his studies occasioned him much trouble; he was slow to learn and what he did learn he retained only imperfectly. The study of Latin was for him particularly difficult.

In his need he turned to the Blessed Virgin and to St. Francis Regis, the Apostle of Vivarais, to whom he had been devoted since childhood. He undertook a pilgrimage to the latter's tomb at Louvesc to beseech his help. His faithful confidence was rewarded and from that time on he experienced fewer difficulties in his studies. When, in after years, Jean was appointed pastor at Ars, he gratefully remembered the saint's assistance and brought his statue into the parish church and zealously promoted devotion to him.

Hardly had Jean begun his studies when an unfortunate obstacle arose. Napoleon I, at that time holding the destiny of France in his hands, needed troops for his Spanish campaign. These were raised by conscription, and notwithstanding the pleadings of his relatives and of several influential persons, Jean was drawn for military service. The sorrow which he experienced at this sudden interruption in his studies was so acute that he became seriously ill and had to be taken to the hospital, first at Lyons and later at Roanne, the troops meantime having departed for the Pyrenees. As a matter of fact it came about that after a long absence from home, Jean was enabled to return to his native village without having performed any actual military services.

In 1812, after close application to his studies, Jean was so far advanced as to be permitted to commence the study of philosophy at Verrieres. He was now in his twenty-seventh year, and there found himself one of two hundred pupils, all younger than he. Another bitter trial now awaited him, for, a few weeks afterwards, he was declared disqualified to take the course in philosophy in the Latin tongue, and with six other students he had to attend this course in the French language.

Not infrequently he was made the butt of his fellow students' ridicule, yet he was never aroused to anger. Instead, these annoyances only served to increase his acts of devotion. Still greater trials, however, were in store for him. Before being admitted into the great seminary of Lyons to make his preparation for Holy Orders, he was required to submit to an examination in philosophy. This took place in the presence of the archbishop and his council. When the questions, presented in Latin, were put to him his memory wholly failed, and in sheer confusion he could answer nothing, so overawed was he by the presence of the distinguished visitors. Accordingly, he alone of all the candidates was dismissed as unfit to enter the seminary. Imagine how hard a blow this must have been to Jean. All his work of the preceding eight years appeared to have been unsuccessful.

In that time of trial Vianney's confidence in God remained unshaken and he was rewarded by finding a friend in the person of his old pastor, Father Bailey, who, better acquainted with the character and qualifications of his protege, induced the authorities to examine Jean privately the following day. This examination was held before the vicar-general of the archdiocese and the regent of the theological seminary, and was so satisfactory that Jean was now permitted to enter the seminary for the course of theology, in 1814.

As an inmate of the seminary his career was remarkable more for the piety of his life than for the brilliancy of his intellect. The regent, however, who recognized Vianney's sterling worth, gave him for his room-mate a fellow student of marked ability who took pains to assist Vianney in his studies, and thus aided, Jean advanced toward the time of his ordination. At that time, 1814, there was a great need of priests and, for this reason, it was planned that Vianney, with other alumni should receive subdeacon's orders in the approaching month of July. But the authorities hesitated. How could they admit to the higher orders one so poorly qualified? This question the vicar-general saw fit to settle for himself, and, after examining Vianney thoroughly, he announced with complacency: "You know as much as many a country pastor."

The vicar-general, however, had previously conferred with the superior of the seminary and had asked him: "Is young Vianney pious? Is he devoted to the Blessed Virgin?" The authorities were able to assure him fully upon these points. "Then," said the vicar-general, "I will receive him. Divine grace will do the rest." Thus, on July 2d, 1814, Vianney received subdeacon's orders and about twelve month's later those of deacon. In August, of the year 1815, he was raised to the dignity of the priesthood by the bishop of Grenoble, representing the archbishop of Lyons, who was at that time in Rome.

Vianney was then twenty-nine years old. The bishop had expressed the hope that the newly ordained would prove to be an efficient laborer in the Master's vineyard. Divine Providence, however, had much more than this in store for the newly consecrated priest, for he was to become a model, whom Holy Church was one day to present to the entire clergy of the Catholic world for imitation.

The Blessed Vianney, in his humility, constantly realized and lamented his imperfections. The sublime ideals of the priesthood and in particular those of a pastor charged with the care of souls living in the world, were ever present to him. Later in life he declared that a true pastor should ever be guided by two principles: (1), he should never permit himself to think that he can accomplish nothing in his parish, no matter for how long a time his efforts may have appeared unfruitful and, (2), he should never consider that he has done enough, no matter how much he may have accomplished.

In order to perfect himself Father Vianney took another course in moral theology from the pious and experienced Father Bailey. To him Jean Baptist Vianney was appointed vicar. He lived with him in the parish house and took a zealous part in his pastor's practices and mortifications. They read the breviary together and, during the day, frequently united in expressions of ardent love to the good God. Together they spent hours at a time in adoration before the Tabernacle. In company with his pastor, Father Vianney took his scanty meal, and his little income passed entirely into the hands of the poor. Articles of clothing which had been given to him for his own use went the same way. He was literally possessed of nothing except the clothes which he wore. With his worthy pastor he made daily visits to the poor and needy of the village and neighborhood, comforting and relieving them as much as possible. It took only a short time for his old friend and pastor, Father Bailey, to realize that he was entertaining a saint.

In December, 1817, Father Bailey was taken from his parishioners by death. It was generally hoped that Vicar Vianney would be his successor, but God had other designs. Before the question was settled, death had removed the pastor of the little village of Ars who had only recently taken charge. Thereupon, the vicar-general of the archdiocese sent Father Vianney there, saying, as he wished him Godspeed: "My friend, you are going to a small parish where very little of the love of God can be seen. You are now to enkindle the flame of Divine charity there!"

Most assuredly the vicar-general, in speaking thus, did not dream that in a few decades the little village of Ars would become a glowing hearth of Divine love, spreading its warmth over the entire country.

CHAPTER II

THE GOOD PASTOR

WHEN Jean Baptist Vianney entered his parish on that winter evening in February, 1818, he quickly realized the religious indifference prevailing there and the contrast in this respect to the kindly and religiously inclined Ecully. Upon his arrival, no one came forward to bid him welcome. The very atmosphere of the neighborhood seemed cold and repellant.

The people of that place, while not positively bad, were for the most part indifferent in the matter of their eternal welfare. Daily Mass was attended by only two or three elderly women. For the most trivial excuse, men neglected Sunday Mass. Not one of them attended Vespers, although at the same time the cafes of the village were crowded. Even the most devout of the women approached the Sacraments but rarely, while the men, through human pride, neglected to make their Easter duty. In fact, one of their number begged the pastor to give him Holy Communion in the sacristy, so that no one might see him.

Servile work of every kind was done on Sunday, and at harvest time the carts and wagons were in use during the entire day "carting souls to hell," as Father Vianney not inaptly expressed it.

Not in a day were these conditions changed. Such a result required many years of effort. In time, however, Divine grace triumphed and the almost unknown parish of Ars became the glorious model for the whole of France. The spirit of religion was revived, public worship restored, the Lord's day unusually respected and observed. The parish formed, as it were, one large-family, in which each member vied with the other in the service of God.

What had the young pastor done to thus transform his parish? He did nothing that any other country pastor may not attempt to do. As his parishioners did not come to him, he went to them in their homes. He was not satisfied with one formal visit but called repeatedly upon his people, as their spiritual or temporal needs seemed to require. He timed his visits for the most part when the family were assembled for the noonday meal. He would enter the living room or stand at the threshold and chat in a friendly manner with the members of the household. Although invited to partake of of their hospitality he never accepted the least refreshment, not even a drink of water. He talked with them about their every day life, their cares and anxieties, their hopes and disappointments.

The people soon perceived that Father Vianney was one of themselves and thus they learned to confide in him and to ask his advice in their temporal affairs. Then, whenever occasion presented, with great aptitude he turned the conversation to things supernatural. At the same time he was never insistent. His manner was always affable, never impatient, never reproving; even when he might justly have given reproof. This gentleness in his manner, which, was only the reflex of the charity in his heart, soon won over his people, who now looked forward to his visits and considered themselves highly honored when he called.

We have already had occasion to notice his defective memory, and how in consequence he was so greatly impeded in the prosecution of his studies. This drawback made itself particularly felt when he came to prepare his sermons. Many a sleepless night did the poor man devote to the preparation of the discourses to be given to his people. But his industry, strengthened by the Divine assistance, conquered, so that, while he never possessed the gift of oratory, he spoke easily, earnestly and convincingly, and when, in after years, the pilgrims poured in to Ars, sometimes as many as 20,000 in a single year, he was able to give his daily instruction from the pulpit without any special preparation and without the embarrassment which he had experienced at the beginning of his priestly career.

In order to make the practice of religion more attractive for his parishioners, he sought to beautify and decorate the little parish church. In this work he was greatly aided by Mademoiselle d'Ars, sister of the

Vicomte d'Ars, who himself generously provided the little church with new vestments and altar vessels.

With the co-operation of his parishioners, who, day by day were learning to appreciate their pastor's solid piety, he built two chapels as an addition to the parish church. One of these he dedicated to St. Philomena, a youthful martyr, whose relics were recovered at Rome in the beginning of the nineteenth century; the other was placed under the invocation of St. John the Baptist, and in it stood the confessional of the cure of Ars, the "Mercy Seat," as it were, of the Almighty, at which untold thousands of souls were reconciled to their Creator.

Despite the fact that the number of his friends and co-workers steadily increased, thus evidencing the fruitfulness of his labors, Father Vianney in truth looked to God alone for success in his undertakings. He realized that he was engaged with the evil spirit in a conflict for the souls of his people and he had read in Holy Writ these words of Jesus Christ: "But this kind (of evil spirit) is not cast out except by prayer and fasting." (Matthew XVII, 20.)

Upon one occasion he recalled these words to a fellow priest who was lamenting that he could obtain no results in his parish, although he had done all in his power to rouse his people from their indifference. Father Vianney said to him: "You have done all in your power? Are you so sure of it? Did you fast and give alms? Did you pray?"

By these questions Father Vianney indicated what were the practices of his own life, which enabled him to obtain results little short of miraculous. His charity was boundless. The food, clothing and other supplies, which the generous Mademoiselle d'Ars sent for the rectory, as a rule, promptly found their way to the poor and needy. Father Vianney actually kept for himself only what was barely sufficient to ward off starvation. Even this modicum was frequently given away, when a poor man came and asked for food.

One evening when Mr. Mandy, the Maire of Ars, came to visit the cure, he found him pale as death and apparently exhausted. Greatly alarmed, he exclaimed: "Are you ill, Father Vianney?" "Oh, my good friend," the latter replied, "you are just in time, I have nothing left to eat." For three days Father Vianney had had no provisions whatever in the house, having bestowed the last of his potatoes upon a poor mendicant. He partook daily of but one meal and that consisted generally of boiled potatoes, which he was accustomed to cook in a quantity sufficient to last through the week, so that oftentimes by Friday or Saturday what remained had become mouldy. When his relatives came to see him, or if he had other visitors, he took pains to have a plain meal provided for them. Under no consideration would he allow any mention to be made of his mortification and self-denial.

As with food so also Father Vianney deprived himself of the various articles of clothing with which he had been supplied. Being accosted on his way home by a poor man whose feet were bare and sore, he divested himself of his own shoes and stockings, gave them to the mendicant, and returned home barefoot.

Vianney was wont to declare jestingly that he had never left his overcoat anywhere. As a matter of fact he did not possess one, thus fulfilling literally our Lord's words: "He that hath two coats, let him give to him that hath none!" (Luke III, 11.). His colleagues were often displeased at his poverty-stricken appearance and regarded his shabby clothes as a reflection upon their dignity. These faultfinders could easily have learned that the patched garments of the hero of brotherly love commanded the respect of all who knew Vianney's real character. Wherever he appeared he was received with the utmost respect and cordially greeted by all.

He offered up to God all his mortifications for the welfare of his people, increasing these exercises habitually as Easter approached, and whenever it was a question of touching the heart of a hardened sinner. He joined prayer to fasting. At two o'clock in the morning he arose and said the night-office of the breviary. At four o'clock he entered the church to visit our Lord in the Blessed Sacrament and then said his Mass. After Mass he

gave instruction in catechism and heard confessions. So steadily was he occupied in this work that he seldom left the church until noon-time. He devoted the afternoons to visiting the sick and spent the rest of the day in the church, where, to the edification of all, he held evening devotions in public.

What could the Lord refuse to such self-sacrificing love? Vianney himself used to say: "I obtained from Him everything that I wanted!"

The progress in the spiritual condition of the congregation at Ars necessarily became known in the surrounding country and Father Vianney's fellow priests of other parishes begged him to help them in the pulpit and confessional. These requests Father Vianney never refused, so that, in the space of two years, he became the real apostle of the cathedral circuit. So great was the success of his spiritual labors that the faithful who desired his assistance no longer waited until he should come again to their parishes, but themselves visited him at Ars. Soon the high road to Ars was filled with pedestrians and vehicles carrying a great number of visitors, and this procession of pilgrims increased when reports were spread of the miracles which took place at Ars.

CHAPTER III

THE "HOUSE OF PROVIDENCE"
AND THE TRIBULATIONS

IN 1825, seven years after Father Vianney had been appointed to the parish at Ars, he resolved upon a new and important undertaking. He wanted to bring together in one home all the neglected poor and orphan children of Ars and the surrounding country, and to provide at one and the same time for both their physical and spiritual needs. Facing the village green there stood a desirable house, which he would gladly have acquired for this purpose. One day he received from an anonymous donor a considerable sum of money for charitable purposes. He immediately betook himself to the owner of the house in question, and without much difficulty was enabled to purchase it. And this was the beginning of the "House of Providence."

As directresses for this home he selected two young women of the parish and placed them in charge, but without imposing upon them any religious vows. The home soon sheltered many little ones, either neglected or homeless, who were fed, clothed and cared for, and whose instruction in the catechism Vianney took upon himself daily. By degrees the grown up parishioners came to assist at these instructions, which took the place of those which had been held in the parish church.

This home was maintained by Father Vianney for twenty-five years. For its financial support he made use of the alms given to him, and it frequently happened that sums of money to be used in charity were transmitted to him most unexpectedly and at times when the home was in greatest need. Relief sometimes came in a manner which excludes the idea of human intervention. Among other incidents observed by many witnesses it is related that one day there was no flour for the day's supply of bread and no money with which to purchase any. Everyone whom Father Vianney approached upon this subject seemed either to be unable or unwilling to relieve him, so that the cure imagined himself almost forsaken.

Never before had he felt so miserable. Then he remembered St. Francis Regis and deciding to seek heavenly intercession, he took the relics of the saint and carried them to the store-room, concealing them under the remnant of grain that lay there. Next day the care-takers of the home came and again reminded the pastor that there was nothing left to eat in the house. Father Vianney, weeping, exclaimed: "Then we must send our poor children away!" Nevertheless he betook himself with one of the care-takers to the store-room and, with great anxiety, opened the door, when, behold the store-room which had been empty was found to be filled with grain.

It was on such an occasion as this that Father Vianney's sanctity manifested itself. Instead of welcoming this public miracle with joyful satisfaction he felt on the contrary, deeply humiliated, because of his having previously given way to discouragement. He hastened to the children of the home and exclaimed in self-accusation "Behold, dear children, I mistrusted the good God. I was about to send you all away, and for this He has well punished me!"

The report of this miraculous supply of food was quickly circulated. The whole congregation visited the store-room; everyone could convince himself of the truth of the matter. Later, Bishop Devie, of Belley, inquired personally into the matter and found the facts to be as above stated.

Now, great graces in the lives of holy persons are never bestowed without great trials, and the good cure was no exception to this rule. During the ten years of his ministry he had suffered from suspicion, distrust and calumny. His enemies had criticised his actions and had held him up to derision. He had even been threatened with violence. Among those who attacked him were some of his own colleagues in the ministry, who were greatly angered because their parishioners flocked in numbers to Ars to ask advice and counsel of one whom they had called the inexperienced and ignorant priest. Of course Father Vianney's own behavior gave no little reason for their disparaging opinion of him, for, in his humility, he had several times declared himself to be a worthless and incapable servant of God, an opinion which undoubtedly he sincerely held.

These aspersions from his colleagues were disseminated among the people, so that many of the faithful, influenced by the mistaken opinion of their spiritual leaders, took upon themselves the liberty of defaming their pastor. Some went further and wrote and left at his door notice containing coarse and dishonorable remarks. To such an extent had these ideas progressed that some persons attributed the furrows with which penitential works had seamed the brow of the humble priest to an immoral mode living.

With touching patience and resignation Father Vianney bore those years of bitterness. His zeal never relaxed for a day, and the interior agony which he suffered was not observable in any of his pastoral duties. At that time he frequently repeated those memorable and beautiful words: "We can do more for God when we perform our duties faithfully, without interior gladness and a certain relish in fulfilling them."

The profound repose of his inner life will appear still more admirable to those who learn what cunning snares were prepared for him at the same time by the arch enemy of the human race.

When news of the diabolical visitations to which Father Vianney was frequently exposed, reached his colleagues, they laughed aloud. They declared that he was a dreamer, whose brain was disordered.

With his accustomed composure the humbled cure bore the derision of his colleagues, and of the faithful who agreed with them. Far from being weakminded, as his associates represented him to be, Father Vianney at first refused to believe that it was the powers of evil that were persecuting him and depriving him of his night's rest in order to render him unfit for his pastoral duties. When the nocturnal rappings became more pronounced, he begged some courageous men of the parish to assist him in discovering the evildoers or thieves, as he at first considered them, whose purpose he thought was to carry off some of the costly articles which had been presented for the parish church. Those men came to keep watch with him, and for many nights in succession they heard the same sounds which Father Vianney had heard, without seeing any person or thing to account for them. Like their pastor they were much wrought up over the strange occurrences.

One winter's night, however, when the rappings upon the front door were louder than usual, the cure sprang from his bed and hurried to the courtyard, believing that he might find traces of the marauder in the freshly fallen snow. But there were no foot prints to be seen. Then Father Vianney no longer doubted that it was Satan that was persecuting him and this conviction removed all sentiments of fear from his soul, for he knew well how to combat the enemy of God.

These violent satanic assaults were kept up against Father Vianney for the space of thirty-five years. That a man so tortured and deprived continually of his needed rest, so enfeebled by the mortifications which he imposed on himself, did not die earlier than his seventy-fourth year, seems almost more miraculous than the inexhaustible activity of his life.

Meanwhile his enemies had advanced a step further in their efforts to render this zealous pastor's position precarious. They calumniated him to the bishop of the diocese of Belley, to which Ars now belonged, saying that their pastor was unfit to be entrusted with the care of souls. The bishop, however, would not condemn the poor priest without a hearing. He sent his vicar-general to Ars and informed Father Vianney that in future he must submit to the episcopal jurisdiction all difficult cases of conscience coming before him as well as the decision he has passed upon them himself. The investigation was welcomed by Father Vianney, and he very soon submitted over two hundred cases. Bishop Devie, of Belley, examined these himself and found that the decisions reached upon the difficult points (excepting only two cases in which his opinion differed), were correct. From that moment he would not suffer anyone to speak, of the cure of Ars as an incapable pastor. About this time, moreover, the bishop personally visited Father Vianney at his house in Ars, and found there a zealous and holy man, instead of the ridiculous figure which the cure's enemies had made him out to be. Speaking one day to his assembled clergy, in regard to the cure of Ars, he said: "Gentlemen, would that you all had a trifle of the foolishness about which you make so merry. It would not prejudice your intelligence in the least!"

Yet, far more than the protection thus afforded by the bishop, did the unalterable humility and amiability of Father Vianney bring these opponents to reason. In the course of a few years this noble character ceased to have any enemies among the clergy. Laymen likewise stopped their calumnies, even if they did not cease their ridicule altogether.

But God had prepared a new trial for His servant. We have already told how Father Vianney had founded and under great difficulties had carried on the home for neglected children called the "The Providence." The time had come when this useful institution was to be taken from his control. The board of education had found fault with the home as being neither a regular school nor a hospital. The clergy criticised its management by lay persons, until at last the bishop was prevailed upon to put the institution in charge of a religious order, and the cure, although sore at heart, subscribed to the deed of surrender in November, 1847. Thereupon the Sisters of St. Joseph from Bourg were put in charge of the institution, which came to be known as a "Free School for Girls." Soon it became evident that this blow, hard as it was, but in which Father Vianney as ever beheld the finger of God, turned out to his profit, for all the powers of his body and mind henceforth were devoted to the single purpose of the conversion of sinners, who kept coming to Ars in ever increasing numbers.

Before we speak further on this point, we must draw attention to an event that took place in the year 1843. In May of that year, Father Vianney became ill as a result of overwork. So serious was his condition that he received the last Sacraments. There was universal sorrow in the village and the church was constantly filled with parishioners who prayed that he might be spared. But the physicians gave no hope. One of them as he touched the cold hand of the motionless figure, exclaimed aloud: "He has only a few moments to live."

The dying man heard plainly the verdict pronounced over him and at that same moment, as he afterwards declared, he was seized with such terror of the supreme judgment of God, that he besought the intercession of the Blessed Virgin and of St. Philomena, and he implored the Almighty through them to vouchsafe to postpone the awful moment of his appearance before Him. His prayers were heard.

To the great astonishment of those present the vitality of the man, sick apparently unto death, returned and, on May 19th, Father Vianney was able to be carried into the church amidst the rejoicings of his children, and there he prayed at length before the Tabernacle. But at this time he made a resolution which, earlier, he could not have carried into effect. His bishop, seeing the great amount of work which had to be performed at Ars, had sent him an assistant priest, to whom, in his humility, Vianney considered himself subordinate and, knowing that there was Someone now to take his place, he decided to retire from his pastoral work and to spend the rest of his "poor life," as he called it, in some remote monastery. To carry out this purpose he planned to flee from Ars under cover of the darkness and mist. But his project was betrayed by his friends at the "Providence" to whom he was obliged to give necessary instructions regarding the future care of the children. Great excitement immediately prevailed among the parishioners and the many visitors, and they quietly surrounded the rectory in order to prevent his escape. The pastor, however, managed to elude them and made his way through a path in the garden which had been overlooked and hastened to his birth-place at Dardilly.

Thereupon the sheep went in search of their shepherd, but as soon as they discovered him in his home he fled farther away, they still following him. At last, moved by the distress which his departure had caused and the appeals made to him by the inhabitants of Ars to return to them, he concluded that it was the holy will of God that he should return and resume the heavy burden of his pastorate, from which he had hoped to be relieved. All thought they had surely won him back, but later on the Blessed Vianney made two other efforts to lay down his pastoral cares and to retire into a monastery, there to work out his own salvation. But God granted the fervent petition of the people of Ars and caused these plans to come to naught.

CHAPTER IV

PILGRIMAGES TO ARS

NOT only to the villagers, but in a greater degree to the pilgrims who journeyed to Ars, Father Vianney's departure would have been particularly disappointing. As early as the period between 1825 and 1830, these remarkable pilgrimages had taken place. So great was the multitude of people who kept coming that increased traveling accomodations had to be arranged between Ars and the outlying country places.

The pilgrims arrived from every province of France; others came from Belgium and England; some from America. At Ars one met bishops and cardinals, prefects of state, university professors, rich merchants, bankers, men and women of ancient and noble lineage, side by side with an innumerable army of priests and religious. As yet the newspapers had not published any account of the wonders accomplished there. Only by word of mouth was the fame of the cure made known, and this unending procession of pilgrims was merely the result of the personal experience of those who had already come under Father Vianney's influence.

With ever increasing wonder the new arrivals observed the great power which that humble priest exercised over souls. Every day in the aisle of the church two rows of men, numbering from sixty to a hundred, awaited their turn to go to confession in the little sacristy. If the question were put as to how long they had been waiting there the answer sometimes was: "since two o'clock in the morning," or, "since midnight, as soon as the cure had opened the church." The stranger would learn with astonishment that men from the highest walks of life had frequently waited patiently a whole day and night, not in order to assist at some great ceremony, but to submit themselves humbly to the guidance of the cure in the matter of the welfare of their souls.

The church was equally crowded elsewhere, and it was no unusual thing to find two hundred women or more waiting their turn to confess their sins. The spectacle of those men and women absorbed in prayer continued from hour to hour and from day to day. As a rule Father Vianney heard confessions daily for sixteen and even eighteen hours and this almost superhuman practice continued for a period of thirty years.

At seven or eight o'clock in the morning the cure said Mass and gave Holy Communion. After Mass he blessed the articles of devotion presented to him at the altar rail, as well as the little children that were brought to him. At eleven o'clock he moved through the crowded ranks of those present and, ascending the pulpit, he delivered a plain but impressive sermon on the truths of holy faith. He who formerly could preach a sermon only under the greatest difficulty, now manifested an imperturbable calm and assurance, for the Divine grace so noticeably inspired his addresses that in many cases, according to the evidence of the different pilgrims themselves, it so happened that his words touched the very ones who, up to that time, had remained in their sins, and, his affecting appeal to them to consider the awful state of their souls, removed the last obstacle to their reconciling themselves to God.

At first, indeed, Father Vianney was greatly distressed when circumstances necessitated his preaching without special preparation; yet, as in this he saw only the will of God, he abandoned himself with complete resignation to the Divine plans, and thus became, although he had no suspicion of it himself, a most eloquent apostle. In his sermons he was accustomed to recall the scenes of his early life as a farmer lad, and he employed the analogies and arguments drawn from external nature and, according to his own statements, it was evident that there was nothing in the visible world that had not reminded him of God and of eternity. Besides these expressive comparisons, Father Vianney's sermons frequently described incidents drawn from his personal experience.

Thus, one day, speaking of lukewarm Christians, he said: "You there behold a tepid soul, which for the most paltry excuse starts to gossip while praying. Does this soul really offer to God the day's work? Does it return Him thanks and glorify Him? Without doubt the lips will speak the words, but for the most part no thought is given to what is said. The soul never ceases to busy itself with the things that are only of this world."

"Again," said he, "we notice a man in church, turning his hat round and round in his hand. Or, we observe in her home a woman, who said grace while cutting bread for the children or while putting wood on the fire, or she interrupts her prayers to call the help."

As a man of the people, Father Vianney knew that in order to hold their attention nothing was so serviceable as to give them a faithful portrayal of every day life. In his discourses he always reverted to the fundamental truths of faith and placed vividly before his auditors for their consideration, the four last things. Ever and anon he would return to the necessity of man's loving God; that this love ought to be as natural to men as song was to the bird. It was impossible for him to preach without referring to the unspeakable joys which arise in the soul of man through a self-sacrificing love of God.

As soon as the sermon was at an end the people hastened to the village green, where the good cure was accustomed to pass on the way to the "Providence" and to his home, delaying on the way to give advice and consolation to those who applied to him. Everyone called him "Father," a title readily admitted by all who observed his kindly manner and still, kinder speech. Father Vianney moved, slowly through the surging throng and, although he was gentleness itself, yet unabashed and obtrusive persons were now and again brought to reason by a quiet though firm answer.

Many an ingenious reply has been recorded of the good cure. A young girl who, from spiritual laziness, had submitted the question of her vocation to the good cure, asked him in a loud tone: "Father, what is my vocation to be?" To which he replied: "My child, your vocation is to get to heaven."

At a glance Father Vianney could recognize innocent souls. It was often observed how he would say suddenly to certain individuals: "Dear child, just go home; you have no need of me." Yet sixteen to eighteen hours daily hardly sufficed to allow him to attend to the distressed souls who knelt in his confessional, since for these above all God had sent the cure of Ars.

Here we arrive naturally at the important subject of the conversions that took place at Ars. Time and again the noble priest would say: "Let us pray for the conversion of sinners!" He declared that prayer for this purpose was one of the most pleasing that could be offered to the good God. Without cessation he himself prayed with this intention and took upon himself all kinds of mortification. His petitions ascended to the throne of God, who, during the thirty years of the cure's life at Ars, was pleased to send innumerable sinners to Ars to be reconciled. Many of these sank at his feet already prepared, for they had heard from others that it was sweet and easy to confess one's sins to the saintly priest and under his guidance, to repent of them with their whole heart.

On one occasion a driver knocked loudly at the door of the cure's house at midnight and asked that his confession be heard at once. Without hesitation, Father Vianney arose and went with him into the church. After he had reconciled him to God Vianney embraced him cordially and gave him some warm clothing, as he noticed the man was suffering from the cold.

With many sinners the workings of grace were decidedly slower. Some had come to Ars out of curiosity, others to unmask the cure, as they thought to do, and to make merry over the "gullible crowd" as the pilgrims were called. But, after closely observing the holy priest for one or two days, they lost all desire to compare him to a "town crier," and it was not long before they joined the crowds waiting for confession.

With still another class it required a direct call of grace. Like St. Vincent Ferrer, Father Vianney had received from God the gift of being able to read clearly into the conscience of a sinner. Hence almost every day it happened that one would see him come suddenly out of the sacristy and advance straight towards a person who had only just entered the church. With a kind and earnest look he would lead him at once to his confessional. Many such penitents acknowledged later that Father Vianney, without more ado, would mention their sins to them beforehand, reminding them especially of those shameful matters in their past life which they might have been tempted to conceal. Thereby he not infrequently removed the last obstacle to complete reconciliation with God.

Among others the following incident is well attested. A certain man, thirty-two; years of age, went to Ars in company with a friend, intending to ridicule Father Vianney. The man had with him his hunting dog, having planned to enjoy the pleasures of the chase in the neighboring fields. At the very moment when the cure was passing across the village square and through the kneeling multitudes, the two friends appeared on the scene. Presently Father Vianney found himself face to face with the curious sportsman pushing through the crowd. After a hasty glance at the dog running at his side, the cure, without further ceremony, said to its owner: "Sir, it were to be desired that your soul were as beautiful as your hound!" The man shamefacedly lowered his head and, shortly after, moved by divine grace, made his confession with copious tears and that same year adopted the life of a religious, in which he persevered until death.

Upon another occasion, among the curious spectators in the church at Ars was a highly educated freethinker, a mocker at religion, of the Voltaire stamp. To please his wife he had accompanied her to Ars, in order, as he expressed it, to have a look at "the old buffoon." With a scornful air he surveyed the crowd praying devoutly in the little church. Suddenly the cure stepped out of the confessional, advanced towards the new arrival, and, with an imposing movement of the hand, requested him to go into the sacristy.

Astonished and confused the unbeliever followed the priest. There Father Vianney sought to bring him to his knees. The latter declared that he had no idea of going to confession, and that he did not believe in it. Father Vianney looked him squarely in the eyes, and under that piercing glance the freethinker sank upon his knees. Then Father Vianney described to him his past life, with surprising accuracy and drew from him the admission that all he had told him was true. The light of faith was forthwith rekindled in the soul of the sinner, who, strongly affected, cried out with violent sobs: "My God, I believe; I adore Thee; I love Thee; and beg of Thee forgiveness!"

Father Vianney dismissed him with the words; "Dear friend, hold yourself prepared; the good God will call you to Himself very soon!" And so it was. Two years later a stroke of apoplexy brought to a sudden end the convert's life.

Besides reconciling sinners with God the indefatigable cure was frequently engaged in the important work of directing souls to the knowledge and attainment of their vocation and in giving other counsel valuable in their spiritual life. Seeking such advice there flocked to Ars, from all parts, bishops and pastors, leaders of religious communities, fathers and mothers of families, young men and young girls in great numbers, all eager to obtain the advice of the good priest. The latter gave his decisions promptly, for he never allowed himself to forget that sinners were waiting for him at his confessional. Many who thus applied declared that Father Vianney, after listening to the first few words, was able to give his advice upon the matter at issue with the fullest intelligence.

Upon one occasion a pastor in the diocese of Autun, presented to the cure for his opinion a very difficult case in moral theology, involving a question of restitution. He received from him such a prompt answer, removing all doubt that, astounded, he asked the cure where he had studied his theology? With a motion of the hand, which conveyed an advice rather than an answer, Father Vianney pointed silently to his prie-dieu.

We have referred to the great number of persons who applied to the cure for advice concerning the religious vocation, but it would be a mistake to suppose that the cure advised young persons indiscriminately to embrace the priesthood or the monastic life. Such was not the case; on the contrary the cure dissuaded many from entering the cloister, although the parties themselves felt strongly attracted to it. In this respect the story of Miss A. C. is instructive.

That lady wished to enter a convent. Her father, who had large property interests in the South of France, wanted her to marry a young man who would become his successor. They agreed to ask Father Vianney's advice and to follow it. This was in the year 1858, a few months before the death of the blessed cure. Father Vianney listened with his accustomed kindness to the young girl's recital, reflected a moment and then exclaimed to the surprised young lady: "My dear child, you ought to marry!" When she referred to her desire to enter a convent, the cure interrupted her, and said again: "Get married, and prove to all that your piety is genuine." Miss C. obeyed and, as the wife of the young man who had asked her hand, was very happy.

At another time a pastor came to him saying that he desired to become a Dominican. Father Vianney exclaimed: "No, my friend, this desire is unfounded; stay where you are." The pastor suggested that as a friar preacher he could be more successful. The blessed cure replied immediately: "Where you are placed there is always more to do than you can really accomplish!"

More than once the result shows how imprudent it was to disregard the counsels of that enlightened man. A certain Felix B. from Coblone, came to Ars on Sept. 8th, 1854, the feast of the Nativity of the Blessed Virgin. As Father Vianney was passing through the throng, which on that day was very great, he noticed the young man, and walked straight towards him. Felix made known to him forthwith his desire of entering a Trappist monastery. "Very well, dear friend," said Father Vianney, "carry out your intention and God will bless you!"

When Felix returned home he felt so faint hearted at the thought of entering an order of such strict observance that he postponed for two years his plan of adopting the monastic life. At last, in 1856, as the call to the life of a religious dominated him, he entered the community of the "Christian Brothers."

But this did not bring him the happiness which he had anticipated. He remained in this congregation for six years, all the while in a state of unrest and discontent. The more he reflected upon his condition the more vividly there stood before his spiritual gaze the image of the cure of Ars (who, meanwhile, had died), and he recalled the advice he had received but had not followed.

After a hard struggle with his own stubborn nature, Felix sought release from the community to which he was attached and asked to be permitted to enter a Trappist monastery which had recently been founded in the arch-diocese. This was accordingly arranged. From that day all unrest vanished and the Trappist monk found peace and contentment in the life to which he had been advised by the cure of Ars.

CHAPTER V

MIRACLES WROUGHT BY THE CURE OF ARS

INNUMERABLE were the miracles worked by the holy man whose history we are relating. They resemble in their marvellous scope and variety, those of the Divine Master, who foretold the accomplishment of wonders greater than His own in the ministry of His faithful servants. The account of the upbuilding of the House of Providence has given us an insight into the power of the holy man who reproduced the scriptural story of the multiplication of the loaves and fishes. We have there seen that often many persons were fed when the larder and the granary were empty. Another phase of the miraculous power of blessed Vianney's prayer to obtain help in time of need, the results of which often gave proof of supernatural intervention, is seen in a good work very dear to him, familiarly known in France as "Fondements." These "Fondements" referred to the establishment of a fund for the perpetual offering of the Holy Sacrifice for some desired end. Blessed Vianney established one thousand annual Masses. The "Fondements" represented a capital of 40,000 francs. Not only did it effect a spiritual good, but going out to needy priests it created in itself a continuous and generous contribution to charity. Some of the miraculous interventions of Providence that touched his heart most deeply are found in his efforts in this direction.

We shall cite but one. A member of the household of Providence relates it: "Once when Father Vianney desired to make a "Fondement" in his church in honor of the heart of Mary, he prayed: O, my mother! if this work is agreeable to thee, procure for me the funds to do it. That same day, after the catechism, he said to us: "I have found 200 francs in my drawer. How good God is!" "Well," exclaimed Jeanne Marie Chaney, "since it is miraculous silver, we must keep some of it." "Yes!" replied the cure, "it is celestial money." Jeanne Marie kept four of the five franc pieces, replacing them by others. She regretted she had not done the same with all the pieces. When, a little later, he wished to increase this "Fondement" Father Vianney prayed again in the same vein, adding, however, the request that the 200 francs must be given to him that evening, or the gift would not be considered an answer to his petition. It was but a little while later, when a benefactor approached him with an offering of 300 francs. His prayer was answered. He took only the sum which he had prayed for." It was in the unceasing war that he waged against the desecration of the Lord's day that his people beheld frequently their saintly pastor's power over the elements. We shall cite an instance:

One Sunday in July there was a full harvest, the wheat bending to the earth. During the High Mass a violent wind arose and threatening clouds gathered; a destructive tempest was apparently about to break. The holy priest entered the pulpit, forbade his people to touch their crops that day, and promised them a continuation of good weather sufficient for the gathering in of the harvest. His prediction was verified; the storm passed over and no rain fell for twelve days.

In the depths of human souls miracles abounded in Ars. For the conversion of sinners the holy cure lived; for them he entered upon his thorny way of heroic penance. His whole life was characterized by prayer, penance and self-abnegation. All counted as nothing if he could win the conversion of his parish, dreaming not of a world to be won from beyond its borders.

His first great conversion was that of a woman prominent in the Jansenist sect for her attachment to error and the indiscreet ardor of her proselytism. She was present during Vespers, in the church of Ars, on a feast of the Blessed Virgin, in the early days of the cure's pastorate. To the surprise of all, she entered the confessional after the service. The words of the holy confessor in the sacred tribunal finished the work that his very aspect alone had begun. Her conversion was thorough and lasting. She withdrew from her former associates and took up her abode in the little village of Ars.

Another miracle of grace, chosen from many, is the following, briefly told:

A learned geologist was led to visit Ars. As a boy he had made his First Communion during the reign of terror. Left an orphan at the age of twelve years he was adopted by an army officer, whom he accompanied to Egypt. His religious experiences had been varied, for he had tested Mohamedanism, Judaism, Protestantism and had been a disciple of Chanel, Pere Enfantine and Cabet. On his first visit to Ars he sat facing the door through which the cure would come to say Mass. His own words tell the result:

"His eyes met mine. It was but a look, yet it penetrated to the depths of my heart, I felt myself crushed under his gaze." After the Mass this man was drawn by an invisible and irresistible force into the sacristy, where stood the confessional. The grace of a return to the faith of his youth was given to him. He died in holy sentiments two years afterwards.

Such spiritual marvels, worked by the Blessed Vianney, were of frequent occurrence. He wept when sinners refused to weep, and they left his feet like other Augustines, to comfort the mother bowed down with sorrow because of their sins. One young man, long lost to his God, had been induced to go to Ars, before leaving for the army. The holy priest singled him, out among the crowd, and beckoned to the young man, who was seized with a sudden trembling. The sacristy door closed upon them and a miracle was wrought there and then on one who had lost his faith, his honor and his home. He came out in tears, remained at Ars to make a retreat, and entered an austere religious order to end his days in heroic penance.

Such are the types of miracles of the spiritual order, the dearest to him, worked by the holy pastor of Ars, whose worst reproach to the hardened sinner was: "What a pity it is! At the hour of death God will say to you: "Why have you offended Me. I who have loved you so much.""

The power to lay bare the hidden sins which the cure's unknown penitent concealed from him, stands forth prominently in his life story and wrought many conversions. So, too, that other power, which divined the future misuse of recovery and sent back the pilgrim, helped, not bodily, but with the healing of patience and resignation, under some long borne affliction. Again, the similar power to see the future augmentation of holiness in a soul under physical affliction and God's will that no cure be wrought; and still another, to see some impending cross awaiting at home a pilgrim, of whom humanly speaking, he knew nothing, and to hasten his departure; or to know by interior sight alone, a cure wrought at a distance. Surely miraculous gifts and all were possessed by the holy cure.

BODILY ILLS MIRACULOUSLY CURED

Through Father Vianney were affected cures of the mentally afflicted, of paralytics from birth or accident, of sufferers from cancer and bronchial affection. There are those whose tongue had never spoken, whose ear had never heard, whose eye had never seen until the holy cure's word had gone forth: "Make a novena to St. Philomena; I will pray with you."

A nervous malady racked the being of Mademoiselle Zoe Pradille and deprived her of the power of walking, of kneeling, of reading and listening to reading and of eating without excruciating pain. Expert medical treatment was secured at home and a thorough test was made of health resorts, all without avail, until at last the pilgrimage was made to Ars and the novena was said, resulting in a complete cure as attested to by a physician who had known the case well for six years out of the eight which the patient had suffered.

A house, during its course of removal, fell and buried under the ruins a little child and her grandmother. The mother of the little one escaped and ran about distracted, while the fruitless search went on. Someone ran to make the accident known to Father Vianney. He knelt first in prayer, then hastened to the spot, blessed the ruins, and stood by encouraging the workmen, who were making the search. The grandmother was rescued unharmed. The child was found after a longer imprisonment in the ruins. She showed not the slightest sign of injury.

A member of the cure's household gave an old cap that the cure had worn to a poor woman, as an alms. The beautiful thought came to her: "The holy cure is a saint. If I have faith, my child will be cured." The boy had an abscess on the head. She put the cap on him. That evening, when she uncovered him to dress the wound, she found that the sore had disappeared. The child had been cured.

"To-day," one wrote from Ars, "we have had a very remarkable cure. It is of a young nun from the Alps whose tongue had been completely paralyzed for three years, after her recovery from typhoid fever. She could converse only by writing on a slate. The day on which she finished her novena, just as she was about to make her thanksgiving after Holy Communion, she felt that her tongue was articulating the acts. She now can speak. I have seen and heard her." The cure of her home parish and the physician who attended her in her convent, testified to her recovery.

One of the remarkable cures, instantly and publicly effected in presence of all the pilgrims, was that of a young man from Pud de Dome who could walk only with difficulty and with the aid of crutches.

"My Father, do you think I will leave my crutches here?" was his oft-repeated question during the novena. On the feast of the assumption he intercepted the holy priest as he came from the sacristy into the crowded church for the evening exercises and again put the question.

"Yes, my friend, if you have faith," was the reply. Instantly the power was given to the young man to walk unaided, and he hastened to St. Philomena's chapel to leave his crutches there. His gratitude was the life-long consecration of himself to God in the institute of the Brothers of the Holy Family.

Miracles of this kind caused the priest considerable embarrassment. He sought to hide from the public eye the marvelous results of his God-given power manifested daily in his parish, His "dear little St. Philomena," who never failed him in his hour of need, heard many plaints from him in which he charged her with working the marvels that were effected through his ministry. Such was the humility of the "wonder-worker" of our own age.

The gift of a medal of St. Philomena was often the preliminary manifestation of miraculous power. This gift was followed by a request that a novena be made to the saint, Father Vianney promising to pray also. The result was frequently the desired miracle, which was in reality the outcome of the cure's powerful pleading with God. Nevertheless, it could easily be laid at the door of his "dear little saint." This was especially so on occasions when the sufferers were not brought to the village or when the cures did not take place until the afflicted ones were far distant from the ordinary scene of the miracles.

A noteworthy instance, in which the good God seemed, as it were, to play into Vianney's hands at times, by allowing St. Philomena to have the full credit of the miracle, was that of the poor wandering musician. He came to the holy cure begging the latter to heal his lame child. After persuading this man to go to confession he blessed him and sent him home, making him promise to mend his evil ways and to cease carrying on an abuse against which the priest waged a relentless war, namely, the village dances, which were held on Sundays and festivals.

When the musician entered his home, he broke his violin and cast the pieces into the fire, to the great dismay of his wife, who saw their family means of sustenance consumed. But his lame child, crying out with joy, leaped across the room to welcome his father. The child was completely cured.

Father Vianney's tenderness was once deeply stirred at the sight of a mother bearing on her back a paralyzed boy of eight years, a cripple from birth. The cure was apparently turning a deaf ear to the mother's repeated appeals for the cure of her child, content with giving them a glance of pity and sympathy and a blessing. Yet, as the result seems to show, his soul must have spoken some word to the soul of the child, audible to none other. At night the mother left the church with a disappointed heart.

While undressing her little son, in a lodging near by, the boy told her she must go out early in the morning to buy him a pair of new shoes. "For," said he, "Father Vianney promised that I would walk to-morrow." Not a word had been spoken to the child, but his mother did his bidding, and put the new shoes on him. The miracle, delayed in the crowded church, was wrought at the moment in the lowly lodging room. The child, crippled from birth, ran to the church, crying: "I am cured, I am cured."

The miraculous power of the cure's sanctity which, during thirty years, attracted considerable attention, could have been welcomed by him for one reason alone, that it helped so much in the aim of his life—the conversion of sinners. That it was the reward not only of his simple faith but of the heroic and unceasing penance which he performed in order to secure the salvation of souls, seems implied in words of his own.

A friend in the priesthood once said to him, when a much needed sum of money had come in an astonishing way: "Tell me, Father Vianney, the way to work miracles." The holy man, with a serious air, replied: "My friend, there is nothing which disconcerts the devil so much, and attracts the graces of God, more than fasting and prayerful watchings." His life, it may be truly said, was one incessant prayer and vigil. A simple peasant has beautifully said: "It is not astonishing that he works miracles. He is a servant of God. God obeys his servants." "They tell us of marvelous things that took place here," said a pilgrim who but echoed the words of many, "but the grand miracle of Ars is the life, so penitent and laborious, of the cure." No miracles showed more clearly his extraordinary gifts and graces than the power which his spirit possessed over his poor emaciated body; and no miracle was greater than his absolute control over his physical state when he seemed on the verge of dissolution, a control that enabled him to bear the over-powering burden of his incessant labors for souls, without sinking under the load. A miracle alone can explain this extraordinary existence.

CHAPTER VI

THE INTERIOR LIFE OF THE BLESSED CURE

IN the preceding chapters we have recounted many things both edifying and interesting in the external life of the pious cure. But for a better knowledge of his noble personality we must look into his inner life. Many readers of these lines have doubtless asked themselves how the cure, in his unremitting labors for others, could have bestowed the necessary care upon his own soul.

Let it be understood that the very moment when the cure seemed to have any leisure for himself, he was more actively engaged in the business of his own spiritual welfare. Then were displayed those beautiful virtues which showed him to be an example of charity and meekness, of voluntary sacrifice and humility. The very glow from his clear eyes revealed the genuine piety by which he was animated. To all who approached him, Father Vianney showed a befitting attention and respect. Indeed, with increasing years, he was even more affable than before.

And yet to what trials was not his patience subjected? Almost daily, as he passed through the village square, people would crowd about him, tug at his soutane and ask questions, which were oftimes trivial, if not foolish. Father Vianney never met importunate persons with so much as a harsh word or a frown. His unchanging kindness toward all earned for him in his life-time the title of the "Good Cure." He was ever considerate of his co-workers, striving to spare them every irksome duty. In order to show his affection he distributed among them his personal belongings, including crosses, medals and relics, which he dearly prized.

For many years before his death he possessed absolutely nothing. He had sold his furniture, books, etc., and had given the proceeds to the poor. The purchasers generally were glad to have him use the articles for which they had given him the money.

Lenient as Father Vianney was towards others, he was correspondingly severe with himself. He was extremely hard upon his own body, which he referred to as his "corpse." After his superiors had prohibited some of the rigorous mortifications to which he was accustomed, he devised other forms of self-denial in respect to his daily food.

During the last decade of his life he was required, by order of his superiors, to take, every morning, at least a cup of milk and a roll. Brother Jerome, who waited upon him, observed that the cure, with his usual desire to practice penance, first ate the dry bread and then drank the milk.

For many years Father Vianney suffered from violent pains which frequently compelled him to shorten his addresses in the pulpit and sometimes even caused him to collapse. If, on such occasions, he were questioned about his illness his only answer was: "Yes, I am suffering a little." Terrible indeed must have been his torture when we consider that his emaciated body, racked with pain, was confined for sixteen or seventeen hours a day, during so many years, in the narrow space of the confessional.

In the winter he suffered greatly from the cold. The north-west wind blowing over the bleak region of the Jura mountains, whistled through the door of the church, which could not be kept closed owing to the constant stream of penitents passing in and out. In summer, conditions were worse, if that were possible, for on account of the location of his confessional, only the air from the farther side could reach it and that was heated and stifling because of the many persons who were gathered there. Frequently, when Father Vianney left the confessional, he was unable to stand erect, being obliged to support himself by leaning against the seats or pillars of the church.

After a day of such work and suffering he was surely entitled to a full night's rest. But no, he often said that with one hour of sound sleep he found himself quite refreshed. Even this one hour, however, was hardly ever allowed him. Like one grievously sick he breathed painfully as he lay on his miserable couch of straw. A cough unceasingly racked his body. He arose every night four or five times, in the hope of getting some relief by walking up and down.

When at last thoroughly exhausted he slept only for a short time. When the hour for rising had come, this poor, feeble septuagenarian with a heroic effort tore himself away from the rest which he had hardly enjoyed and began the work of another day as long and as trying as that which had gone before.

To these corporal sufferings was added spiritual anguish of the bitterest kind. In his own life the cure was a saint, chaste, magnanimous and faithful, and yet, day after day, he had to listen in the confessional to an endless recital of sins against those virtues. Loving God as he did, with his whole soul, he could not but suffer when listening to the recital of most grievous offences committed against the Divine Majesty. His heart was torn thereby and not infrequently his anguish manifested itself in a flood of tears.

One day while giving instructions in catechism, he cried out: "There is no one in the world more unhappy than the guardian of souls. How does he spend his time? In hearing how the good God has been offended and His love rejected! Like St. Peter the poor priest is ever to be found in the court of Pilate. The Divine Saviour is always before his gaze, derided, scorned and reviled. Some sinners are spitting upon His countenance, others rain blows upon His defenceless head; still others crown Him with thorns and scourge Him until the blood flows. He is buffeted about, thrown on the ground and trampled upon. He is crucified and His heart is transpierced. Alas! had I known what it meant to be a confessor, instead of going to a seminary I would rather have fled to a Trappist Monastery."

It would have been some consolation and encouragement if the poor cure's humility had allowed him to rejoice at the tremendous success of his spiritual labors. But no matter what wonderful effects his ministry produced, he always regarded himself as most incapable of discharging his priestly duties as they should be performed. With unaffected sympathy did he speak of his "poor soul," his "poor corpse" his "poor sins" and his "poor misery," praying that God in His goodness would bear with them. Without his humility, Father Vianney undoubtedly would not have become a saint. How otherwise could he have withstood for years the enthusiastic veneration of the thousands who were the witnesses of his holy life.

One day, when Bishop Devie, of Belley, in the ardor of conversation, gave him the title of the "holy cure," Father Vianney in despair ejaculated: "Oh, what a misfortune for me! Your reverence even is deceived in me." He was more than surprised when, in August, in the year 1855, he was nominated a "Knight of the Legion of Honor." Of course he never wore the badge nor availed himself in any way of the distinction. Against the onrush of a multitude of corporal and spiritual anxieties and cares he sought consolation in prayer.

It has remained almost completely a secret what supernatural consolations were vouchsafed to the blessed cure. On that subject he always preserved a strict silence. He prayed practically throughout the whole night, for his sufferings, as mentioned above, allowed him only a few minutes rest at a time. What he recommended to others in the catechism lessons, he himself constantly practiced. He was wont to say, for instance: "See now, dear children, should you wake up during the night, go quickly in spirit before the tabernacle and say to our Saviour: "Here am I, O Lord, I adore Thee, I praise Thee, I thank Thee, I love Thee and with the Angels let me keep Thee company.""

During the day all his spare time was devoted to prayer. In visiting the sick his thoughts were always with God. But his prayers were of the most simple kind. He favored simplicity in every action.

In the church, before the Blessed Sacrament, the pious cure's sense of the Real Presence was so vivid that a colleague, who noticed his radiant look, regarded him with astonishment, thinking Father Vianney with his corporal eyes, beheld Someone there. This intuition of the Divine Presence the pious man referred to, one day, saying: "That is faith when we speak to God as a fellow man!"

Despite the ardor of his desire for God's blissful vision, he had to struggle for many decades in the exile of this life, persevering in work and prayer. Only when his venerable age and increasing infirmities disabled him from further laboring in the conversion of sinners, did our Divine Lord see fit to take this soul to Himself. The cure was then in his seventy-fourth year.

CHAPTER VII

DEATH AND BEATIFICATION
OF THE BLESSED CURE

IT was in the summer of 1859, that the venerable cure showed that his energies were nearly spent. He was then heard repeatedly to exclaim: "Alas, the sinners will kill the sinner."

On Friday, July 29th, after having as usual spent from sixteen to seventeen hours in the confessional, he returned to the rectory completely exhausted. He sank into a chair saying: "I can do no more." The priest who saw him, immediately put him to bed. On the following morning his illness was so pronounced that a fatal termination was feared. In the village and among the numerous visitors to Ars the greatest sorrow was felt. For three days the church was crowded with the faithful, praying that their cure might not be taken from them.

The cure did not join his prayers to those of his people for he felt that his last hour was approaching. On Friday evening he received the last sacraments. He shed tears of love when the Holy Viaticum was brought to him and as Extreme Unction was being administered. For the last time he blessed all who were present as well as his whole parish. On Wednesday morning he smilingly acknowledged the greeting of his bishop, who had hurried to his bedside. On Thursday, Aug. 4th, at two o'clock in the morning, while his friend and assistant, the Abbe Monnin, was saying the prayers for the dying and had just uttered the words: "May the holy Angels of God come forth to meet him and conduct him into the city of the Heavenly Jerusalem," the loving soul left his frail body to be received, as we may devoutly hope, into the presence of the Divine Master, whom he had served so long and so faithfully.

The demise of the good cure was immediately made known to the sorrowing community. On Saturday of that week the interment took place. Almost six thousand persons, many of whom came from afar, attended the funeral. Three hundred priests accompanied the remains to the grave. The bishop of Belley, in his eulogy, selected his text from the office of the feast of the Saints and Confessors: "Well done, thou good and faithful servant, enter into the joy of thy Lord." All present understood the sentiments which prompted the selection of that particular text and trusted that their hope would not be disappointed.

Rarely has a process of beatification been set in motion so quickly as was that of John Baptist Vianney. Hardly forty-five years had elapsed since the remains of the deceased were laid at rest, under the pulpit of his parish church, when the Holy See announced its decision permitting the beatification process to be introduced.

As early as Oct, 3d, 1874, Pope Pius IX, after examining the various writings and biographical notices relating to the deceased and published by reliable contemporaries, conferred on the humble cure the title "Venerable Servant of God." On June 21st, 1896, Pope Leo XIII, presiding, the last session of the commission took place, which was to pronounce upon the saintly merits of the venerable cure. The favorable conclusion which everyone expected was announced by Cardinal Parocchi. On Aug. 1st, of that year, Pope Leo XIII, issued a decree reciting the honors paid to the humble cure of Ars and his own personal admiration for his exalted virtue.

Seven years later, in 1903, the same Pope called a session of the commission to consider the testimony and reports relative to the miracles which had taken place at the tomb of the departed. This session, however, was not held, for on the day which had been appointed the venerable pope lay at the point of death and soon after, viz., on July 20th, of that year, the Catholic world had to mourn the passing away of its spiritual head.

The happy distinction, however, of being able to glorify the humble country curate had been reserved by God for one who himself had been formerly a plain country curate. On Aug. 4th, 1903, at the very hour, when at Ars they were celebrating a solemn High Mass on the forty-fourth anniversary of the death of John Baptist Vianney, another solemn ceremony was taking place at Rome, viz., the election of the former village cure of Salzano, later

Cardinal Sarto, patriarch of Venice, to the Papacy, who chose for himself the title of Pius X.

As early as Jan. 26th, 1904, the new supreme pontiff presided at that session of the cardinals over which his illustrious predecessor had intended to preside. Two cases in particular were presented for examination. One was a question of the sudden cure of the youthful Adelaide Joly, and the other, that of little Leo Roussat. The latter, after a violent attack of epilepsy, in the year 1862, had to be carried to the grave of the late cure. One of his arms hung crippled at his side; his power of speech was gone, and his breathing so difficult that he was unable to retain the saliva in his mouth. After a short time spent in prayer at the grave of the cure he was removed. The hand formerly crippled was now able to give alms to the poor and the boy recovered the use of his limbs and walked about. At the conclusion of the novena he was able to speak without further trouble.

In Feb., 1861, the girl Adelaide, owing to a malignant swelling of the arm, had been given up as incurable by the doctors in the Lyons hospital. Then one of her relatives who possessed a piece of linen, which had belonged to the cure of Ars, laid it upon the affected arm. In prayer they besought the intercession of the venerable servant of God to obtain relief for the suffering girl. To the astonishment of the doctors the swelling was suddenly reduced in a few hours and the arm was restored to its normal condition.

After the counsel of cardinals had pronounced a favorable opinion in respect to the miraculous nature of these cures, a papal decree, dated Feb. 21st, 1904, declared these facts sufficiently established to justify the beatification of the venerable man.

The Holy Father himself gave unrestrained expression to the joy which he felt when he was enabled to admit into the ranks of the blessed one who, according to his own words, had been for many years a shining example to him.

PRAYERS

LITANY AND NOVENA PRAYER

IN HONOR OF Saint John B. Marie Vianney, CURE OF ARS. (FOR PRIVATE DEVOTION.)

LITANY

Lord, have mercy on us. Christ, have mercy on us. Lord, have mercy on us.

Christ, hear us. Christ, graciously hear us.

God the Father of Heaven, have mercy on us.

God the Son, Redeemer of the world, have mercy on us.

God the Holy Ghost, have mercy on us.

Holy Trinity, one God, have mercy on us.

Holy Mary, pray for us.

Blessed John Marie, pray for us.

B. J. M., endowed with grace from thine infancy, pray for us.

B. J. M., model of filial piety, pray for us.

B. J. M., devoted servant of the Immaculate Heart of Mary, pray for us.

B. J. M., spotless lily of purity, pray for us.

B. J. M., faithful imitator of the sufferings of Christ, pray for us.

B. J. M., abyss of humility, pray for us.

B. J. M., seraphim in prayer, pray for us.

B. J. M., faithful adorer of the Most Blessed Sacrament, pray for us.

B. J. M., ardent lover of holy poverty, pray for us.

B. J. M., tender friend of the poor, pray for us.

B. J. M., penetrated with the fear of God's judgment, pray for us.

B. J. M., fortified by Divine visions, pray for us.

B. J. M., who wast tormented by the evil spirit, pray for us.

B. J. M., perfect model of sacerdotal virtue, pray for us.

B, J. M., firm and prudent pastor, pray for us.

B. J. M., inflamed by zeal, pray for us.

B. J. M., faithful attendant on the sick, pray for us.

B. J. M., indefatigable catechist, pray for us.

B. J. M., who didst preach in words of fire, pray for us.

B. J. M., wise director of souls, pray for us.

B. J. M., specially gifted with the spirit of counsel, pray for us.

B. J. M., enlightened by light from Heaven, pray for us.

B. J. M., formidable to Satan, pray for us.

B. J. M., compassionate with every misery, pray for us.

B. J. M., providence of the orphans, pray for us.

B. J. M., favored with the gift of miracles, pray for us.

B. J. M., who didst reconcile so many sinners with God, pray for us.

B. J. M., who didst confirm so many of the just in the way of virtue, pray for us.

B. J. M., who didst taste the sweetness of death, pray for us.

B. J. M., who dost now rejoice in the glory of Heaven, pray for us.

B. J. M., helpful to all those who invoke thee, pray for us.

B. J. M., patron of the clergy, pray for us.

Lamb of God, who takest away the sins of the world, Spare us, O Lord.

Lamb of God, who takest away the sins of the world, Hear us, O Lord.

Lamb of God, who takest away the sins of the world, Have mercy on us, O Lord.

Christ, hear us. Christ, graciously hear us.

Pray for us, Blessed John Marie, That we may be made worthy of the promises of Christ.

LET US PRAY

Almighty and merciful God, who didst make the Blessed John Marie admirable in his pastoral zeal and in his constant love of penance, grant us the grace, we implore Thee, to win for Christ, by his example and intercession, the souls of our brethren, and to attain with them everlasting glory—O, Blessed John Marie, incomparable laborer in the field confided to thee, obtain for the Church the realization of Jesus' desire. The harvest is abundant, but the laborers are few. Pray to the Master of the harvest to send faithful laborers into His vineyard. O, Blessed John Marie! Intercede for the clergy. May thy patronage, and thy prayer multiply the real vocations to the priesthood. May the Holy Ghost grant thee emulators; may He give us Saints! Through Christ, our Lord. Amen.

PRAYER TO BLESSED VIANNEY

I thank Thee, my God, for the grace of this novena to Thy blessed servant, Vianney. I beg of Thee, first, that I may learn the singular virtues of this blessed man—his piety, mortification, poverty, love of God and our neighbor. Let me become, in this way, a useful member of the human family. I have, O Lord, prayed to Thy blessed servant Vianney, that he may pray for me and my intention. (Here mention the intention.)

PRAYER TO BLESSED VIANNEY

I thank Thee, my God, for the grace of this novena to Thy blessed servant, Vianney. I beg of Thee, first, that I may learn the singular virtues of this blessed man—his piety, mortification, poverty, love of God and our neighbor. Let me become, in this way, a useful member of the human family. I have, O Lord, prayed to Thy blessed servant Vianney, that he may pray for me and my intention. (Here mention the intention.)

Many graces have been known to have been granted to those who have prayed with this spirit. Even miracles have been wrought by Thee, O God, in approval of this devotion. Encouraged by the merits of the life of the Blessed Vianney, I beg Thee, O Lord, to obtain for me the grace and favor of this novena, through Jesus Christ, our Lord. Amen.

NOVENA IN HONOR OF BLESSED JOHN BAPTIST VIANNEY

Many graces have been known to have been granted to those who have prayed with this spirit. Even miracles have been wrought by Thee, O God, in approval of this devotion. Encouraged by the merits of the life of the Blessed Vianney, I beg Thee, O Lord, to obtain for me the grace and favor of this novena, through Jesus Christ, our Lord. Amen.

FIRST DAY:—FAITH

On this first day of the novena we shall consider the faith of this holy man. A lively faith is necessary in order to please God. We believe every word which God has spoken by His Holy Church. We must practise this faith also in works. Faith without works is dead. Without works it would be only an empty assertion that we believe. In a firm unflinching faith Blessed Vianney lived and died and became a saint.

PRAYER FOR FAITH

Pour into my soul, O God, through the intercession of the Blessed Vianney, pastor of Ars, a deep lively heartfelt faith! That faith will be my salvation, as it was the salvation of all the saints who are now in Heaven. Amen.

Then is said the Litany to the Saint Vianney and the prayer. In these days of frequent Communion, it were well if Holy Communion could be received at the beginning of the novena and also at the end. Better still, if it could be received every day during the novena.

SECOND DAY—CHRISTIAN HOPE

Consider the blessings of Christian hope. It is a trust in God, in His Providence, a lively, filial, trustful submission to the will of God, knowing that God will ordain things to His greater glory and to our spiritual benefit. What consolation is found in a Christian hope! How sweet it is! We cannot be disappointed if we trust in God, Who cannot deceive. Hope is our spiritual life and the principle of our active perseverance in it. How dreary is the world without hope! How glorious life becomes with hope! God puts hope into our hearts.

PRAYER FOR HOPE

Give me, O Lord, that hope which raised the spirit of Blessed Vianney, that hope which gave him patience in long suffering. He did all with the hope that Thy glory would be enhanced. Infuse into my heart the desire to do good work for Thy sake.

THIRD DAY—THE LOVE OF GOD

On the third day we shall consider the love of God. We must love God above all things, live in love, continue in love unto the end. Love the Son of God, Jesus Christ, love the Church, the Spouse of our Lord. The love of God will bring us to Heaven. God will give us everything if we love Him. It is so reasonable to love God; in fact, man is a fool if he does not love God. It is our religion, our happiness and our supreme blessing. It is our very Heaven, here upon earth. The happiness of Heaven, commenced in this world even imperfectly, will be continued for all eternity, if we persevere to the end.

PRAYER FOR THE LOVE OF GOD

O my God, I love Thee with my whole heart, and above all things because Thou, O God, art the Sovereign Good and for Thine own infinite perfections art most worthy of all love.

FOURTH DAY—THE LOVE OF OUR NEIGHBOR

This day will be given to the consideration of the love which we should have for our neighbor. Let us impress the love of our neighbor deeply on our mind. It is so very important. It is second only to the love of God. You cannot do anything pleasing to God unless you do it out of a motive for the love of God or for our neighbor. Those have been the greatest human beings who loved God above all things and their neighbor as themselves.

PRAYER TO OBTAIN THE LOVE OF OUR NEIGHBOR

My dear Jesus, lover of all mankind, teach me to love my neighbor as Thou didst love even Thine enemies. Blessed Vianney was Thy faithful follower in the practice of this virtue. He loved the souls of men. Let me also imbibe, from a devotion to him, the same love for souls.

FIFTH DAY—HUMILITY

The great virtue of our blessed saint was humility. Let us try to imitate and understand this virtue. We will find some good souls who never think much of themselves. They want to be always in the background. They do not want to be considered at all. Nevertheless they are always doing good. These are precious in the sight of God.

PRAYER FOR HUMILITY

O sweet and humble Jesus, give me also the precious virtue of humility, which Thou didst give so abundantly to Thy servant Vianney, so that I also may be pleasing in Thy sight and pleasing before man. No virtue is so attractive as humility. Thou, O Lord, exaltest the humble. To be great in Thy sight and approved by Thee is the object of my desire.

SIXTH DAY—LOVE OF POVERTY

Love of poverty is an active sincere love. The lack of possessions, the desire not to have any, giving to the poor what we have, or what we do not need, is poverty. Practice self-denial. Save to give to the poor, to build hospitals, orphan asylums, churches. Have Masses said for the poor suffering souls in Purgatory.

PRAYER FOR POVERTY

Thou hast said, O Lord, "Blessed is he who understands the poor." Let me have that knowledge. It is the practical way to show my love for my neighbor in distress. Let me also, like Thyself, be a good Samaritan, doing good and relieving want. Not only should I be poor in spirit, but I must also love to be poor in fact, for the poor are the brethren of Christ.

SEVENTH DAY—MORTIFICATION

This day shall be devoted to the virtue of mortification. Put away the comforts of eating and drinking, the extravagance of living, personal luxuries. Live simply and like a poor man. Be simple in dress, but be well dressed. Be abstemious at your table. Especially guard against over indulgence in drink. Abstemiousness in drink is a very commendable virtue. Deny yourself many things that are unnecessary. Do not yield to all the promptings of the appetite. Be temperate.

PRAYER TO OBTAIN THE GRACE OF MORTIFICATION

Thou hast commanded the mortification of the flesh from the beginning, O Lord. From the beginning, the desires of the flesh have been the bane of a good life. When shall Thy grace, O Lord, inspire me with some degree of that firmness and faithful adherence to Thee. Suffer not my heart to be overcome by that inconstancy which is so natural to it, nor allow my life to be a perpetual succession of evil practices and infidelities. Grant that my heart may be all Thine, at all times and forever. And that by mortification I may merit eternal happiness.

EIGHTH DAY—PRAYER

We must pray all the time. Every act must be a prayer. The spirit of prayer must be in our whole Christian life. We must pray if we want to do anything great in the spiritual life. A life without prayer is a most barren period of time. Prayer is the intimate converse with God. Our Saint was always intimately united to God in prayer. Blessed Vianney never ceased praying.

PRAYER FOR A TRUE SPIRIT OF DEVOTION

How sweet, O Lord, to breathe only Thy love and to say to Thee with my whole heart: My God and my all! Grant that words may enter into my soul! do then, impress them upon my mind and my heart so that I may understand and practice them. Let me be devoted to prayer. Make it a delight to converse with Thee. Let me pray for everything I need and before every undertaking, so that with prayer every work may begin and with prayer be happily ended. Thou art my Saviour. May I possess Thee in prayer here on earth and mayest Thou be my portion for all eternity in Heaven.

NINTH DAY—DEVOTION TO MARY

On the last day of the novena we must try to learn and begin to cultivate a devotion, which appeals to the heart of every Catholic, that is, the devotion to the Mother of God. What is a Catholic life without love to Mary! How dark and dreary is a life without the spiritual consolation of the Communion of the Saints! In short, have a great devotion to Mary. Pray to her with confidence like one that has a right to be heard and a right to address her. Love Mary with the sincerest affection. Let not a day pass without having said a prayer to her. Say your beads every day. Wear the scapular in her honor. Go to Confession and Holy Communion on her feast days. Perform many little acts of religion from the motive of love to the Blessed Virgin.

PRAYER TO MARY

My dear Saviour, Jesus Christ, Son of the Virgin Mary, grant me the grace to love Thy mother. This grace is such a distinction, a grace of salvation, which I must have by all means. Hail holy queen, Mother of Mercy, our life, our sweetness and our hope. To thee do we cry, poor banished children of Eve. To thee do we send up our sighs, mourning and weeping in this valley of tears. Turn thou, most gracious advocate, thine eyes of mercy towards us, and after our exile show unto us the fruit of thy blessed womb, O most loving, most pious and sweet virgin Mary. Pray for us, O holy Mother of God, that we may be worthy of the promises of Christ.

CATHOLIC WAY PUBLISHING
PAPERBACKS AND E-BOOKS

True Devotion to Mary: With Preparation for Total Consecration
by Saint Louis De Montfort
   5" x 8" Paperback: ISBN–13: 978-1-78379-000-5
   6" x 9" Hardback: ISBN–13: 978-1-78379-004-3
   Kindle E-Book: ISBN–13: 978-1-78379-001-2
   EPUB E-Book: ISBN–13: 978-1-78379-002-9

The Secret of the Rosary by Saint Louis de Montfort
   5" x 8" Paperback: ISBN–13: 978-1-78379-310-5
   Kindle E-Book: ISBN–13: 978-1-78379-311-2
   EPUB E-Book: ISBN–13: 978-1-78379-312-9

The Mystical City of God by Venerable Mary of Agreda
   Popular Abridgement
   5" x 8" Paperback: ISBN–13: 978-1-78379-063-0
   Kindle E-Book: ISBN–13: 978-1-78379-064-7
   EPUB E-Book: ISBN–13: 978-1-78379-065-4

The Imitation of Christ by Thomas a Kempis
   5" x 8" Paperback: ISBN–13: 978-1-78379-037-1
   Kindle E-Book: ISBN–13: 978-1-78379-038-8
   EPUB E-Book: ISBN–13: 978-1-78379-039-5

My Daily Prayers by Catholic Way Publishing
   5" x 8" Paperback: ISBN–13: 978-1-78379-027-2
   Kindle E-Book: ISBN–13: 978-1-78379-028-9
   EPUB E-Book: ISBN–13: 978-1-78379-029-6

The Three Ages of the Interior Life: Prelude of Eternal Life
by Reverend Reginald Garrigou-Lagrange O.P.
   Volume One
   5" x 8" Paperback: ISBN–13: 978-1-78379-296-2
   Kindle E-Book: ISBN–13: 978-1-78379-297-9
   EPUB E-Book: ISBN–13: 978-1-78379-298-6

   Volume Two
   5" x 8" Paperback: ISBN–13: 978-1-78379-299-3
   Kindle E-Book: ISBN–13: 978-1-78379-300-6
   EPUB E-Book: ISBN–13: 978-1-78379-301-3

✚ **CATHOLIC WAY**
    P U B L I S H I N G

WWW.CATHOLICWAYPUBLISHING.COM
LONDON, UK
2013